HAL•LEONARD
INSTRUMENTAL
PLAY-ALONG

AUDIO
ACCESS
INCLUDED

PLAYBACK+
peed • Pitch • Balance • Loop

CLARINET

CHRISTMAS CLASSICS

Audio arrangements by Peter Deneff

To access audio visit:
www.halleonard.com/mylibrary

Enter Code
1676-6092-3606-2923

ISBN 978-1-4950-7055-6

HAL•LEONARD®
CORPORATION
7777 W. BLUEMOUND RD. P.O. BOX 13819 MILWAUKEE, WI 53213

T0056097

In Australia Contact:
Hal Leonard Australia Pty. Ltd.
4 Lentara Court
Cheltenham, Victoria, 3192 Australia
Email: ausadmin@halleonard.com.au

Visit Hal Leonard Online at
www.halleonard.com

ANGELS WE HAVE HEARD ON HIGH

CLARINET

Traditional French Carol

BRING A TORCH, JEANNETTE, ISABELLA

CLARINET

17th Century French Provençal Carol

COVENTRY CAROL

CLARINET

Traditional English Melody

FUM, FUM, FUM

CLARINET

Traditional Catalonian Carol

GO, TELL IT ON THE MOUNTAIN

CLARINET

African-American Spiritual

GOD REST YE MERRY, GENTLEMEN

CLARINET

Traditional English Carol

HERE WE COME A-CAROLING

CLARINET

Traditional

THE HOLLY AND THE IVY

CLARINET

18th Century English Carol

I SAW THREE SHIPS

CLARINET

Traditional English Carol

JINGLE BELLS

CLARINET

Words and Music by
J. PIERPONT

O COME, ALL YE FAITHFUL

CLARINET

Music by JOHN FRANCIS WADE

O HOLY NIGHT

French Words by PLACIDE CAPPEAU
English Words by JOHN S. DWIGHT
Music by ADOLPHE ADAM

CLARINET

SILENT NIGHT

CLARINET

Words by JOSEPH MOHR
Music by FRANZ X. GRUBER

STILL, STILL, STILL

CLARINET

Salzburg Melody, c.1819

16

WHAT CHILD IS THIS?

CLARINET

16th Century English Melody